First World War
and Army of Occupation
War Diary
France, Belgium and Germany

7 DIVISION
Divisional Troops
220 Machine Gun Company
18 March 1917 - 30 November 1917

WO95/1646/3

The Naval & Military Press Ltd
www.nmarchive.com
Published in association with The National Archives

Published by

The Naval & Military Press Ltd

Unit 10 Ridgewood Industrial Park,

Uckfield, East Sussex,

TN22 5QE England

Tel: +44 (0) 1825 749494

www.naval-military-press.com

www.nmarchive.com

This diary has been reprinted in facsimile from the original. Any imperfections are inevitably reproduced and the quality may fall short of modern type and cartographic standards.

© **Crown Copyright**
Images reproduced by permission of The National Archives, London, England, 2015.

Contents

Document type	Place/Title	Date From	Date To
Heading	WO95/1646/3 7 Division 220 Machine Gun Company May-Nov 1917		
Heading	220 Machine Gun Coy. May 1917 Nov 1917		
Heading	7 Div. 220 M.G. Coy. March 1917		
War Diary	Le Carve France.	18/03/1917	24/03/1917
War Diary	Acheux	25/03/1917	25/03/1917
War Diary	Mailly-Maillet	25/03/1917	27/03/1917
War Diary	Puisieux-Au-Mont	27/03/1917	28/03/1917
War Diary	Courcelles Le Comte	29/03/1918	31/03/1918
War Diary	Courcelles	01/04/1917	30/04/1917
Heading	7th Div. 220 M.G. Coy. May 1917		
War Diary	Courcelles	02/05/1917	05/05/1917
War Diary	Mory	06/05/1917	16/05/1917
War Diary	Courcelles	17/05/1917	31/05/1917
Heading	7th Div 220 M.G. Coy. June 1917		
War Diary	Courcelles	01/06/1917	24/06/1917
War Diary	Mory	25/06/1917	26/06/1917
War Diary	Behagnies	27/05/1917	30/05/1917
Heading	7th Div 220 M.G. Coy. July 1917		
War Diary	Behagnies	01/07/1918	24/07/1918
War Diary	Mory	25/07/1917	31/07/1917
Heading	7th Div 220 M.G. Coy. August 1917		
War Diary	Mory	01/08/1917	09/08/1917
War Diary	Ransart	10/08/1917	28/08/1917
War Diary	Pas En Artois	29/08/1917	30/08/1917
War Diary	Beauvoorde	31/08/1917	31/08/1917
Heading	7th Div. 220 M.G. Coy. September 1917		
War Diary	Beauvoorde	01/09/1917	04/09/1917
War Diary	Hazebrouck	05/09/1917	13/09/1917
War Diary	Arques	14/09/1917	15/09/1917
War Diary	Westbecourt	16/09/1917	27/09/1917
War Diary	Wizernes	28/09/1917	29/09/1917
War Diary	Westoutre	30/09/1917	30/09/1917
War Diary	Chateau	30/09/1917	30/09/1917
Heading	7th Div. 220 M.G. Coy. October 1917		
War Diary	Chateau Segard	01/10/1917	12/10/1917
War Diary	Zevecoten	13/10/1917	19/10/1917
War Diary	Camp 50 (Westoutre Area)	20/10/1917	24/10/1917
War Diary	Lock 8	25/10/1917	30/10/1917
War Diary	Blairinghem	31/10/1917	31/10/1917
Miscellaneous	20th Infantry Brigade. 2nd Infantry Brigade. 91st Infantry Brigade. 220th M.G. Company.	20/10/1917	20/10/1917
Heading	7th Div. 220 M.G. Coy. November 1917		
War Diary	Blaringhem	01/11/1917	12/11/1917
War Diary	Fauquembergues	13/11/1917	14/11/1917
War Diary	Canlers	15/11/1917	26/11/1917
War Diary	Sabbion	27/11/1917	29/11/1917
War Diary	Villaga	30/11/1917	30/11/1917
Operation(al) Order(s)	220 Machine Gun Coy Movement Order No. 2		
Miscellaneous	220 Machine Gun Company. Move Order No. 4	16/11/1917	16/11/1917

Miscellaneous	220 Machine Gun Company. Move Order No. 5
Miscellaneous	220 Machine Gun Company. Entrainment Orders.

WO 95/1646/3 7 Division

③ 220 Machine Gun Company

Mar – Nov 1917

7th Division

200 Machine Gun Coy Nov 1917
Nov 1917 -
2nd Remount Squadron
appx 1918

WAR DIARY

220
M. G. COY.
March 1917.

7th Div:

WAR DIARY 220 M. G. Coy.
or
INTELLIGENCE SUMMARY
(Erase heading not required.)

Army Form C. 2118.

Vol 1

Place	Date	Hour	Summary of Events and Information	Remarks and references to Appendices
Le Havre France	1917 18th Mar	7 am	Eight officers and 115 O.R. disembarked from S.S. Antrim and proceeded to No 1 Rest Camp.	
"	19th Mar	8 am	Two officers, 31 O.R. and 54 mules with Coy Transport disembarked from S.S. Huntscraft and proceeded to No 1 Rest Camp.	
"	21st Mar	-	Two O.R. admitted to Hospital.	
"	22nd "	-	One O.R. admitted to Hospital.	
"	24th "	-	Two O.R discharged from Hospital.	
"	"	9.33 pm	Coy entrained.	
ACHEUX	25th	9 pm	Coy detrained. Arrival reported to 7th Division. Marched to billets in MAILLY-MAILLET	
MAILLY-MAILLET	25th "		Arrival reported to 22nd. Brigade.	
"	26th "	10.5 pm	Orders received for Company to proceed to PUISIEUX-AU-MONT.	
"	27th "	10.30 am	Coy left MAILLEY-MAILLET.	
PUISIEUX-AU-MONT	27th "	3.30 pm	Arrival at PUISIEUX-AU-MONT reported to 7th Division.	
"	28th "	1.30 am	Orders received from 7th Division to proceed to COURCELLES LE COMTE.	
"	"	10.30 am	Coy left PUISIEUX-AU-MONT.	

WAR DIARY or INTELLIGENCE SUMMARY

Army Form C. 2118.

(Erase heading not required.)

Place	Date	Hour	Summary of Events and Information	Remarks and references to Appendices
PUISIEUX-AU-MONT	1917 28th Nov	12.30 pm	Company arrived at COURCELLES LE COMTE and went under canvas.	
COURCELLES LE COMTE	29th "	11-15 am	Instructions received from Division to reconnoitre the ground between the villages of SAINT LEGER and VRAUCOURT with a view of holding, with eight guns, the front of the forward artillery and guarding same.	
"	"	4.30 pm	Ground reconnoitred and positions chosen, in co-operation with artillery.	
"	30th "	4.30 pm	Positions previously chosen now occupied and consolidated.	
"	"	—	Section Commanders visited and satisfactory reports received.	

L.O. Springfield
Capt.
O.C. 220 M.G. Coy

WAR DIARY 220 M.G. Company
INTELLIGENCE SUMMARY
April

Place	Date	Hour	Summary of Events and Information	Remarks and references to Appendices
COURCELLES	April 1		Situation normal in the line	
	2		Reserve line ST. LEGER – VRAUCOURT reconnoitred in conjunction with O.C. 22 Coy. 91 Coy.	
	4		1 O.R. admitted Hospital	
	4.		Orders rec.d. from Division for 8 guns to be withdrawn from the line.	
	5		8 guns withdrawn by 9 A.M.	
			Orders rec.d. from Division to attach 2 guns to each of the 22nd & 35th Bdes R.A. for Anti-Aircraft defence.	
			No 4 Section detailed & guns placed in position by 3 P.M.	
			1 O.R. admitted Hospital	
			1 O.R. Discharged Hospital.	
	7.		35th Bde RA moved forward. Anti Aircraft guns moved in co-operation.	
			2 Lt. G.L. Carter wounded.	
			30 O.R. joined from Base Depot as reinforcements.	
	8.		Preliminary warning to be ready to move forward.	
	9.		1 O.R. admitted Hospital	
	10.		2 O.R. joined from Base Depot as reinforcements.	
			Coy placed on short notice to move	

WAR DIARY or INTELLIGENCE SUMMARY.

Army Form C. 2118.

(Erase heading not required.)

Place	Date	Hour	Summary of Events and Information	Remarks and references to Appendices
COURCELLES	11		No further orders re move received. Training proceeded with. 1 O.R. admitted Hospital.	
	12.		Training with limbers. No 4 Section relieved in line by No 2 Section	
	13.	6 PM	Orders received from Division to see D.M.G.O. 62nd Div. with a view to arranging to assist 62nd Division in the capture of BULLECOURT.	
		7 PM	D.M.G.O. 62nd Division seen & arrangements made to place 8 guns in the cutting N.W. of ECOUST. & to place barrage beyond BULLECOURT from Zero to + 1 hour.	
	14.	9 AM	O.C. Coy & No 1 & 3 Section Commanders went forward to reconnoitre line.	
		1 PM	8 Guns & gun teams moved up to MORY under LT. BRETT. Information received that attack was postponed. Coy bivouacked at MORY.	
	15	8.30 AM	Information received operations postponed till 17th. D.M.G.O. 62nd Division seen & arrangements made that the 8 gun teams should move back to COURCELLES.	
		10.30 PM	Message recd. from D.M.G.O. 62nd Division asking for 2 Sections to be at MORY by 11 AM 16/4/17. 2 LT. J. ROBINSON joined from Base Depot.	

WAR DIARY or INTELLIGENCE SUMMARY.

Army Form C. 2118.

(Erase heading not required.)

Place	Date	Hour	Summary of Events and Information	Remarks and references to Appendices
COURCELLES	16.		2 Sections reached MORY at 9 A.M. Operation indefinitely postponed. Sections returned to COURCELLES. Arrangements made with Division that they would inform Company when date was more definitely fixed. 2 LT. J.L. WATSON joined from Base Depot.	
	17.		Kit inspections & repacking of Limbers.	
	18.		No 2 Section relieved in line by No 3 Section. Relief complete by 10 P.M. 3 O.R. admitted to Hospital.	
	19.		Training with limbers & pack animals.	
	20.		Range constructed & No 1 & 4 Sections fired on Range.	
		6 P.M.	Orders received from Division to place two guns in ST LEGER — VRAUCOURT defensive line to guard approaches to ST LEGER from N.E.	
	21.		No 1 Section had the two guns in position by daylight & positions oats falling 1 O.R. killed in action.	

WAR DIARY
or
INTELLIGENCE SUMMARY.
(Erase heading not required.)

Army Form C. 2118.

Place	Date	Hour	Summary of Events and Information	Remarks and references to Appendices
COURCELLES	22		Orders received from Division for 2 more guns to be placed on 2nd Defensive Line. 2 Guns of No 1 Section were in position by 5.0.P.M. No 4 Section Rifle Shooting on Range. Most of shooting bad, owing to newly joined Drafts having had practically no experience of shooting	
	23.		Training. Chiefly Pack Work.	
	24.		1. O.R. admitted Hospital.	
		11.0.AM	Limbers Packed for Open Warfare & inspected by G.O.C. Division	
			1. O.R. joined from Base Depot.	
	25		Training with Pack Animals.	
		3.30 PM	Paraded with 91st Brigade for Gas Demonstration. Small Box Respirators found to facilitate movement of troops & the giving of Orders. Transport & H. wiress inspected by O.C. Div. Train.	

WAR DIARY or INTELLIGENCE SUMMARY

Army Form C. 2118.

(Erase heading not required.)

Place	Date	Hour	Summary of Events and Information	Remarks and references to Appendices
COURCELLES	26		No 3 Section relieved in line by No 4 Section. Relief completed by 4.0.P.M. 2. O.R. admitted Hospital.	
	27		A/C.S.M Wright attached from 91. Company. Training proceeded with.	
	28		—	
	29		No 3 Section - Firing on Range. 2nd in command visited all guns + emplacements. 2 O.R. discharged Hospital. 1 O.R. admitted Hospital.	
	30		No 1 Section relieved in line by No 2. Relief complete 4.30 P.M.	

L.O Springfield Capt
O.C. 220 M.G Coy

WAR DIARY

220
M.G. COY.
May 1914.

7th Div:

WAR DIARY or INTELLIGENCE SUMMARY

220 M G Coy — **Vol 3**

Army Form C. 2118.

Place	Date	Hour	Summary of Events and Information	Remarks and references to Appendices
COURCELLES	May 1st		Kit inspection No.1 Section. No.3 Section tactical scheme	
"	2nd		1. O.R. Special leave to U.K. 2. O.R. reinforcements joined from base Depôt. No.3 Section left camp 11.AM & moved to MORY. No.2 Section withdrawn from defensive line & concentrated at MORY by 5.P.M. Nos. 2 & 3 Sections left MORY at 7.30 P.M. & proceeded to cutting N.W. of ECOUST & made preparations to assist 62 Division in attack on BULLECOURT at dawn next morning. Advanced transport H.Q. established at MORY under Lieut Brett.	
"	3rd	3.45 A.M.	Barrage put down by Nos. 2 & 3 Sections in conjunction with 62nd Div attack for one hour. These guns then formed a defensive line in case of counter attack.	
"	4th		1 O.R. admitted to hospital. 2. O.R. wounded. 2 guns of No.1 Section sent forward from COURCELLES to do anti-Aircraft work at Div H.Q. at MORY. No 4 Section relieved No 1 on battery defence line by 4 guns of 201 Coy. M.G.C. & concentrated at MORY. No.2 Section relieved by 4 guns of 208 Coy M.G.C. & moved to MORY. No. 3 Section relieved by 4 guns of 212 Coy. M.G.C. This section then took over 4 Gun positions on battery defence work from 201 Coy	

WAR DIARY or INTELLIGENCE SUMMARY

Place	Date	Hour	Summary of Events and Information	Remarks and references to Appendices
COURCELLES	May 4th		This relief was made very difficult owing to the fact that the Coy was relieved by three different Coys instead of the Div any of the relieving Division	
"	5th	2.P.M.	The Coy H.Q. moved to MORY under Lieut MOORE. M.C. ~~No 1 Section relieved No 3 Section on Battery defence line No 88~~. No 4 Section occupied defensive line from VRAUCOURT to MORT-HOMME.	
MORY	6th		No 3 Section relieved by No 1 Section on Battery Defence Line. No 3 Section then relieved No 4 Section on Defensive Line. On relief No 4 Section moved to ECOUST to dig in preparatory to assisting 7th Div on its attack on BULLECOURT by barraging fire. One instructions received on 5th inst from Division O.C. & Lieut Durrant reconoitred neighbourhood of ECOUST with a view of choosing possessions from which 8 guns of 91st M.G. Coy & 8 guns of 22nd M.G. Coy could also assist attack by barraging fire. O.s.C. 91 & 22 Coy seen & arrangements made that they should fire from embankment N.W of ECOUST from ZERO + 60. at the rate of 1 belt every three minutes. One O.R. discharged to Hospital.	

WAR DIARY
or
INTELLIGENCE SUMMARY.
(Erase heading not required.)

Army Form C. 2118

Place	Date	Hour	Summary of Events and Information	Remarks and references to Appendices
MORY.	7th	AM 3.40	Barrage put down as arranged.	
		5.00	No. 4 Section relieved 8 guns of 91st M.G. Coy & 8 guns 22nd M.G. Coy. & formed a defensive line.	
		6.P.M.	Arrangements made that No. 4 Section should be relieved by 213 M.G. Coy.	
		6.30	Information received that relieving Coy would be 212 Coy & not 213 as stated.	
		8.0 P.M.	Orders received from 7th Division to concentrate 8 guns at MORT. HOMME forthwith. These guns to come under orders of G.O.C. 20th Inft Bgde. on arrival. 2 guns of No. 2 Section left camp at 8.30 P.M. No 3 Section withdrawn from their positions and concentrated at MORT. HOMME by 9.30 P.M. O.C. made MORT HOMME Adv Coy H.Q.	
		9.0 PM	Verbal instructions received from Bgde Major 20th Bgde to send forward 2 guns to Railway Embankment N.E. of ECOUST.	

WAR DIARY or INTELLIGENCE SUMMARY.

Army Form C. 2118.

Place	Date	Hour	Summary of Events and Information	Remarks and references to Appendices
MORY.	MAY 7	8 P.M.	and two more directly they were available.	
		9.15 PM	Lieut Sargent went forward with 1st two guns	
		9.45	Lieut Robinson " " " 2nd " "	
		12 M.N	Positions reported occupied ~~by Robinson~~.	
	8	5 AM	Subsection No 4 Section relieved Subsection No 2 Section on A/A work in Camp.	
		8.30	Subsection No 2 moved up to MORT HOMME	
			Situation in the line normal.	
			2 O.R. reinforcements	
			2 O.R. wounded	
	9	8 AM	2 i/c took over from OC at MORT HOMME.	
			Situation in the line normal.	
	10	1 AM	Gas alarm sounded. All men in Camp woken up & gas sentry posted.	
		1.30 AM	No sign of gas & camp resumed normal conditions.	
			~~No Section relieved No 4 Section on Battery defence~~	
			1 O.R. admitted Hospital	

WAR DIARY or INTELLIGENCE SUMMARY.

Army Form C. 2118.

Place	Date	Hour	Summary of Events and Information	Remarks and references to Appendices
MORY	10	8 P.M.	No 1 Section withdrawn from Battery defence line. No 4 Section relieved subsections of Nos 2 & 3 Sections in the line. Relieved teams reached camp at 5 AM 11/5/17.	
		11 AM	2/Lt. Bailey with 12 OR & 1 gun reinforced No 20 M.G. Coy in BULLECOURT & was relieved by No 91 Coy during the night 10th/11th.	
	11.		8 OR returned to Base Depot as inefficient. 1 OR joined from Base Depot. 1 OR wounded.	
	12.		1 OR returned to 91 M.G. Coy on ceasing to be employed as A/CSM 2 OR wounded. Adv. Coy HQ under 2 i/c moved back to MORY.	
	13		MORY shelled by enemy during morning. Sections in Camp refitting & organising.	
	14		No 1 Section relieved No 4 Section in line. 2 OR wounded.	
	14	2 P.M.	Orders received from Division to withdraw guns in position on Railway Embankment.	

WAR DIARY or INTELLIGENCE SUMMARY.

Army Form C. 2118.

Place	Date	Hour	Summary of Events and Information	Remarks and references to Appendices
MORY	15	3 AM	No 1 Section returned to Camp.	
			1 O.R. wounded.	
		4.45 AM	"Stand to" order recd from Division.	
		9.30 AM	Orders recd. from Division to move eight (8) guns to MORT HOMME & report to 91 I.B.	
		10	Recd verbal orders to move two guns to Railway Embankment with the object of stopping an enemy advance from the direction of the CRUCIFIX should he attempt to do so.	
			Two guns to be moved to cellars in ECOUST & remaining four guns to be in reserve at MORT HOMME. Report centre under 2/Lt Robinson established in cellars occupied by two guns.	
		3 PM	2/Lt Bailey i/c 2 guns in ECOUST recd. orders to move up at dusk to positions on Railway Embankment.	
			Situation in line quiet. Shelling below normal.	
			Lt. J.R. MOORE granted leave to Paris U.P.A.	
			1 O.R. returned from Cold Shoeing Course.	
			O.O. No 154. recd stating that Dn. Gn. in the line would be relieved on the night 16/17th. On relief Coy to be concentrated at COURCELLES.	
		12.45	G.C. 416. recd from Division stating that Coy would relieve 58th Division on Anti-Aircraft defence in back areas namely VALHEUREUX & ACHEUX. Relief to be completed by night 17th May.	

WAR DIARY or INTELLIGENCE SUMMARY

Place	Date	Hour	Summary of Events and Information	Remarks and references to Appendices
MORY.	16.		Coy. H.Q. moved to COURCELLES under 2 Lt Durrant. No 1 Section left Camp at 10AM to proceed on A/A duty as laid down in G.O. 716 overleaf.	
		6PM	No 4 Section relieved at MORT HOMME by 214 M.G. Coy. & on relief moved to COURCELLES. Our 4 Guns on Railway Embankment relieved by 214 M.G. Coy & on relief moved to MORY. 2 Lt Robinson & report centre withdrawn to MORY. Signalling lamp used to call up limbers from MORT HOMME to ECOUST as needed by out coming teams. This saved keeping transport at ECOUST longer than necessary.	
COURCELLES.	17.	11AM	Details who stayed at MORY for night 16/17th left for COURCELLES under O.C. O.C. visited A/A guns at ACHEUX & VAL HEUREUX.	
	18.		Reorganising & equipping.	
	19.		Lt Brett & 1 O.R. to A.S.C. Course with 7th D.W. Train	
	20.		Sunday.	
	21.		4 O.R. reinforcements from Base Depot.	

WAR DIARY or INTELLIGENCE SUMMARY.

Army Form C. 2118.

(Erase heading not required.)

Place	Date	Hour	Summary of Events and Information	Remarks and references to Appendices
COURCELLES	21		2/Lt Baselow + 3.4.O.R. to V Corps Lewis Gun School for A/A Course	
"	23	9.30AM	Inspection by V Corps M.G.O. Orders red from V Army through Division for DOULLENS Station to be protected by M.Gs. 1.O.R. proceeded on leave to U.K.	
"	24		Lieut Baselow + 4.O.R. returned from 5th Corps Lewis gun A/A course. Lieut Durrant + 13.O.R. proceeded to DOULENS on A/A duty. 1.O.R. proceeded on Leave to U.K.	
"	25	9.30	No 2 Section under Lieut Baselow went to DOUCHY with Lieut Bailey to reconnoitre trenches in view of taking part in tactical scheme.	
		12.30 8.30 pm	No 3 Section left with 5 limbers and rations under O.C Coy to take part in tactical Scheme at DOUCHY + AYETTE	
"	26	11.0 AM	Coy returned under Lieut Moore from tactical Scheme at DOUCHY.	
"	27	9.30	No 3 Section proceeded to ACHEUX + VALHEUREUX to relieve No 1 Section. Company on A/A duty.	
"	28	4.30	No 1 Section returned from ACHEUX + VALHEUREUX.	
"	30	9.30	Company programme of Training carried out. O.C. left to visit Sections at ACHEUX + DOULENS. Coy allotted Baths 10 to 12. AM.	
		3.00	Lieut Bailey proceeded to DOULENS with one O.R. to relieve Lieut DURRANT of command of A/A duties.	

WAR DIARY
or
INTELLIGENCE SUMMARY.
(Erase heading not required.)

Army Form C. 2118.

Place	Date	Hour	Summary of Events and Information	Remarks and references to Appendices
COURCELLES	MAY 31	2:30	14. O.R. rejoined from Base depôt. Lieut Durrant rejoined company from DOULENS & took over duties of 2/i.c.	
		4.00	Lieut J.R. MOORE proceeded to take over command of 971 M.G. Coy.	

31/5/17.

H Henry Full Capt
O.C. 220 M.G. Coy

WAR DIARY

220 M. G. COY.

June 1917.

7th Div:

WAR DIARY 220 Machine Gun Company

~~INTELLIGENCE SUMMARY~~

JUNE Vol 4

Army Form C. 2118.

Place	Date	Hour	Summary of Events and Information	Remarks and references to Appendices
COURCELLES	June 1	6am	1 O.R. to Cooking Course at Albert	
			1 O.R. to Hospital	
	2	7am	Company under O.C. went to the MIRAUMONT RANGE. Returned 6 p.m.	
	3	10am	O.Co inspection.	
		2pm	12 O.Rs of No 4 Section under Lt. RICHARDSON proceeded to DOULLENS to relieve 12 O.Rs of No 4 Section on a/a duty. 2nd Lieut. BAILEY remained at DOULLENS.	
	4	9am	Company under O.C. went to the MIRAUMONT RANGE. Returned 6.30 p.m.	
		2 p.m.	12 O.Rs of No 4 Section under Corporal ORME returned from DOULLENS	
			1 O.R. to hospital	
			1 O.R. rejoined from hospital	
	5		Company Programme of training carried out.	
			1 O.R. to hospital	
			1 OR rejoined from hospital	
	6	9am	Company under O.C. went to the MIRAUMONT RANGE. Returned 6.30 p.m.	
	7	2 pm	No. 2 Section under 2nd Lieut. Sargent left Camp (26 ORs) to relieve a/a Gun Teams at ACHEUX and VALHEUREUX. 2nd Lieut BLEAKLEY & 1 O.R. went to ACHEUX by road with one limber and G.S. Wagon.	

WAR DIARY
or
INTELLIGENCE SUMMARY.

(Erase heading not required.)

Army Form C. 2118.

Instructions regarding War Diaries and Intelligence Summaries are contained in F. S. Regs., Part II. and the Staff Manual respectively. Title pages will be prepared in manuscript.

Place	Date June	Hour	Summary of Events and Information	Remarks and references to Appendices
COURCELLES	7	1.30 pm	2/Lieut ROBINSON and 2 O.Rs returned to camp from ACHEUX to prepare for Course at CAMIERS. 1 O.R. to Cold Shoeing Course	
	8	2 pm	2/Lieut ROBINSON, 4 N.C.Os and 1 O.R. left camp to go to Course at CAMIERS.	
		2.15 pm	SERGT. WRIGHT with 19 O.Rs returned from VALHEUREUX and ACHEUX.	
		8 pm	2/Lieut BASELOW returned to camp with limber and G.S. Wagon.	
	9	9 am	Company under O.C. went to MIRAUMONT RANGE. Returned at 6.30 p.m.	
			2 O.Rs returned off leave to U.K.	
	10	9 am	G.O.C. Division interviewed C.S.M. LESTER and PRIVATE DOUGLAS and recommended both for commissions.	
		9.30 am	O.C. went by Corps M.G.O's car to visit guns at ACHEUX, VALHEUREUX and DOULLENS. Returned at 7 pm.	
		10 am	O.Cs inspection of COMPANY.	
			1 O.R. to Hospital	
			1 O.R. from Hospital	
			1 N.C.O. from V Corps School of Instruction.	
			LIEUT BRETT returned from A.S.C. Course	
		2 pm	1 O.R. left Coy. for BOULOGNE Transportation Troops Depôt	
	11		Work carried on as per programme. 1 O.R. admitted to hospital	
	12		Work carried on as per programme.	

WAR DIARY
or
INTELLIGENCE SUMMARY.

(Erase heading not required.)

Army Form C. 2118.

Instructions regarding War Diaries and Intelligence Summaries are contained in F. S. Regs., Part II. and the Staff Manual respectively. Title pages will be prepared in manuscript.

Place	Date June	Hour	Summary of Events and Information	Remarks and references to Appendices
COURCELLES	13		Work carried on as per programme. 1 O.R. to Hospital.	
	14		Work carried on as per programme. 1 O.R. to Hospital. 1 O.R. evacuated.	
	15		Work in morning as per programme. O.C., Lt. DURRANT & 2/Lt. IBBERSON reconnoitred ground for tactical scheme.	
		5pm	2/Lieut BASELOW and 2/Lieut WATSON each took his sub-section to DOUCHY to reconnoitre ground with view to tactical scheme.	
		9pm	2/Lieut IBBERSON and remainder of No. 1 and No. 3 Sections went to DOUCHY.	
		9.30pm	O.C. and LIEUT DURRANT went to AYETTE and then to DOUCHY.	
	16	9am	Company under O.C. returned to CAMP. 1 O.R. to Hospital. 1 O.R. discharged from Hospital.	
	17	10am	O.C's inspection	
		2pm	No. 1 Section under 2/Lt. IBBERSON and WATSON left camp to go to ALBERT to mount all four guns for A/A duty in relief of the ANZACS. 2/Lt. BAILEY and sub-section of No. 4 returned from DOULLENS having been relieved by 2/Lt BLEAKLEY and his sub-section of No. 2. 2/Lt. BLEAKLEY's sub-section were previously relieved at ACHEUX by the ANZACS. 1 O.R. to hospital.	
	18		2 ORs to hospital. 1 O.R. to Divisional Physical Training & Bayonet fighting Course.	

WAR DIARY or INTELLIGENCE SUMMARY.

Army Form C. 2118.

Place	Date	Hour	Summary of Events and Information	Remarks and references to Appendices
COURCELLES	19		Work carried on as per programme. Lieut. DURRANT & 2/Lieut. BASELOW went on 4 days leave to PARIS. 2 O.Rs. to Hospital	
	20	2.30 p.m	Work as per programme Lectures by O.C. Company	
	21	9 a.m.	Company under 2/Lieut. BAILEY went to BUCQUOY for tactical scheme. O.C. followed later. 1 O.R. to hospital. 3 O.Rs. reinforcements.	
	22		Work as per programme 1 O.R. to hospital.	
	23		Work as per programme. 2/Lieuts. IBBERSON & WATSON returned from ALBERT (relieved by 208 Coy) 1 O.R. from hospital. 1 O.R. from Cookery Course.	
	24	2 p.m. 10.45 p.m.	Company moved to MORY under O.C. 4 guns of No. 4 Section to the line S.E. of ECOUST (2nd Lieut. BAILEY and 21 O.Rs) 2 guns of No. 1 " " " " N.E. of " (2nd Lieut. WATSON and 11 O.Rs) 2 guns of No. 1 " " " " N.W. of " 2 guns of No. 3 " " " " N.W. of " } 2/Lieut. IBBERSON and 27 O.Rs. These guns got into position to give enfilade barrage fire to support proposed attack by 33 DIVISION at 11.50 a.m. on the 25th JUNE. Two officers arrived back from PARIS leave.	
MORY	25		Cleaned up Camp.	

WAR DIARY or INTELLIGENCE SUMMARY.

Army Form C. 2118.

(Erase heading not required.)

Instructions regarding War Diaries and Intelligence Summaries are contained in F. S. Regs., Part II. and the Staff Manual respectively. Title pages will be prepared in manuscript.

Place	Date	Hour	Summary of Events and Information	Remarks and references to Appendices
MORY	25	11.48 am	Wire received indicating that proposed attack by 33rd DIVISION was postponed. 2 ORs from hospital. 1 OR to School of Cookery at ALBERT.	
	26	2 am	2/Lieut. IBBERSON reached camp with his four guns and 27 ORs.	
		10 am	Company moved to BEHAGNIES. 1 O.R. left Company to join CADET UNIT in ENGLAND.	
BEHAGNIES	27		Work in new camp.	
		2 pm	O.C. and 2/Lieut BASELOW reconnoitred line and visited 2/Lieuts BAILEY and WATSON and their gun positions.	
	28		Orders received for 1 section (4 guns) to give enfilade barrage fire to support proposed attack by 33rd DIVISION at 8.50 on 29.6.17.	
		11.30 pm	2/Lieut Ibberson and 26 ORs left camp to get into position for this attack. MAJOR MATHESON appointed D.M.G.O. and O.C. 220 M.G Coy. Major Matheson went up to the line with Captain Springfield and returned at 11 pm. 1 O.R. to hospital.	
	29		Major Matheson officially took over command of 220 M.G Coy. Barrage carried out.	
		10 pm	Capt. Springfield went up with rations & visited gun positions. returned 1 a.m. 1 O.R. to hospital. 1 o.r. from hospital	
	30	2 am	2/Lieut IBBERSON and 26 ORs returned from line.	

WAR DIARY or INTELLIGENCE SUMMARY.

Army Form C. 2118.

Place	Date	Hour	Summary of Events and Information	Remarks and references to Appendices
BEHAGNIES	30	4 p.m.	2/Lieut ROBINSON and 5 O.Rs returned from M.G. Course at CAMIERS. 1 O.R. to Veterinary Course at ABBEVILLE. 1 O.R. to hospital. Authority received appointing Lieut DURRANT Second in Command of 220 M.G. Coy from 31.5.17.	
		10 p.m.	2/Lieut BASELOW and 11 O.Rs went up to the line to relieve 2/Lieut WATSON and his two gun teams on the embankment N.E. of ECOUST.	

K. Springfield Capt
for O.C 220 M.G. Coy

220 M. G. COY.

July 1917

WAR DIARY

7th Divi:

WAR DIARY or INTELLIGENCE SUMMARY

220 MG Coy
JULY 1917
Vol 5

Army Form C. 2118.

Place	Date	Hour	Summary of Events and Information	Remarks and references to Appendices
BEHAGNIES	1	4am	2/Lieut. WATSON and 11 ORs returned to camp from the line	
		9.30pm	2/Lieut ROBINSON and 19 ORs went up to the line to relieve 2/Lieut BAILEY and 21 ORs in four gun positions S.E of ECOUST.	
			1 OR to Hospital	
	2	2am	2/Lieut BAILEY and 21 ORs returned from line	
		3pm	Capt. SPRINGFIELD went up to visit guns of Mr. Robinson & Mr. Barlow	
	3	3.30am	O.C. visited guns on Divisional front.	
			Intimation received that the DOULLENS and VALHEUREUX guns might be relieved by Lewis guns.	
	4		Work in Camp. 1 OR from Hospital. The Captain visited Corps guns returned 12 midnight	
	5		Information received that A/A guns at Valheureux & Doullens might be relieved by Lewis guns of the 24th Manchesters (Pioneers).	
	6	5pm	O.C. and Captain went up line & returned 9 p.m. 1 OR to Hospital	
	7		Information received that Lewis guns of 24th Manchesters were relieving A/A gun teams at Doullens and Valheureux.	

WAR DIARY or INTELLIGENCE SUMMARY.

Army Form C. 2118.

Place	Date	Hour	Summary of Events and Information	Remarks and references to Appendices
BEHAGNIES	7	6p.m.	2/Lieuts. BAILEY and WATSON with 25 ORs of No. 4 Section went up the line to dig four anti-aircraft emplacements W. of ECOUST	
		9.30p.m	Guns for these positions taken up under Capt. SPRINGFIELD. Instructions sent to Mr. ROBINSON and Mr. BASELOW as to barrage in connection with proposed raid by 20th BRIGADE on the night of the 8th-9th	
	8	2 a.m.	Sgt. ROGERS and 9 ORs returned from line. Information received that proposed raid by 20th BRIGADE was cancelled but 2/Lieut. SARGENT had been returned and was returning to Coy. H.Q. with his two gun teams on the 9th	
		12.30 p.m	2/Lieut. BLEAKLEY and 12 ORs returned from VALHEUREUX	
	9	1 a.m.	2/Lieuts. ROBINSON and BASELOW with 20 ORs returned from line, having been relieved by 20th M.G. Coy.	
		1 p.m.	2/Lieut. SARGENT & 8 ORs returned from DOULLENS	
			2 ORs to Hospital. 1 OR Reinforcement	
	10	6 a.m.	Capt. SPRINGFIELD visited emplacements of No. 4 Section	
		2 p.m.	Working party under Sgt. ROGERS to Mr. WATSON's positions	

WAR DIARY or INTELLIGENCE SUMMARY.

Army Form C. 2118.

Instructions regarding War Diaries and Intelligence Summaries are contained in F. S. Regs., Part II. and the Staff Manual respectively. Title pages will be prepared in manuscript.

(Erase heading not required.)

Place	Date	Hour	Summary of Events and Information	Remarks and references to Appendices
BEHAGNIES	10	3.30 pm	2/Lieut. BLEAKLEY went to 91st M.G.Coy H.Q. to see gun positions on 91st Brigade front which it had been arranged that 220 M.G.Coy should take over.	
		9 pm	2/Lieut. SARGENT and 14 ORs and 2 guns went up line to get into these positions	
	11	1.30 am	Mr. Sargent returned to camp.	
	10	9.30 pm	Working party under CAPT. SPRINGFIELD to gun positions of No. 4 Section	
	11	3 pm	CAPT. SPRINGFIELD visited all 220 M.G.Coy. gun positions – returned 7.30 pm.	
	12		C.S.M. LESTER left Company to go to U.K. for training as a Commissioned officer.	
			Arrangements made for 2 guns of 220 M.G.Coy. to be placed on 91st BRIGADE front	
		4 pm	2/Lieut. SARGENT visited these 2 positions with O.C. 91 M.G.Coy.	
		9 pm	11 ORs with 2 guns went up line to occupy these two positions	
		7.30 pm	Working party of 7 ORs to 2/Lieut. BAILEY	
		"	" " " 7 ORs to 2/Lieut. ~~WATSON~~ BLEAKLEY	
	13	7.30 pm	" " " 7 ORs to 2/Lieut. BLEAKLEY	
		9.30 pm	2/Lieut. ROBINSON & 25 ORs. of No. 3 Section went up the line to get four guns into position on railway embankment N.E. of ECOUST	

WAR DIARY or INTELLIGENCE SUMMARY.

(Erase heading not required.)

Army Form C. 2118.

Place	Date	Hour	Summary of Events and Information	Remarks and references to Appendices
BEHAGNIES	13		for barrage in conjunction with proposed raid by 20th Brigade on night of 14/15th. 1 O.R. from veterinary course at ABBEVILLE. Instructions sent 2/Lieut BLEAKLEY regarding barrage by his guns in conjunction with proposed raid by 91st Brigade on the night of 14th-15th. CAPTAIN SPRINGFIELD visited all 220 Boy. guns in line.	
	14	6p.m.	Captain SPRINGFIELD visited all guns of 220 Boy. in the line.	
		8p.m.	2/LIEUT SARGENT went up line to No 3 Sections positions to help with barrage. Ammunition carrying party of 6 O.Rs. to Mr BLEAKLEY. No 3 Section guns fired from Zero till Zero + 3 & from Zero plus 12 till Zero + 22. No 2 Sections 2 guns on embankment fired from Zero till Zero + 30. 2/Lieut. BLEAKLEY took one gun forward & fired directly on enemy front line on flank of raiding party of 91st Brigade. Total rounds fired 15,250. 1 O.R. from School of Cookery ALBERT.	
	15	4 a.m.	2/Lieuts. SARGENT & ROBINSON and 24 O.Rs returned to camp from line. 1 O.R. left in line in charge of guns etc.	
		7.30 a.m	Captain SPRINGFIELD returned from line.	
		2 p.m.	2/Lieut IBBERSON & 1 O.R. visited Mr BLEAKLEY's gun positions.	

WAR DIARY or INTELLIGENCE SUMMARY.

Army Form C. 2118.

(Erase heading not required.)

Place	Date	Hour	Summary of Events and Information	Remarks and references to Appendices
BEHAGNIES	15	5.30	Carrying party of 20 ORs went up line to carry out guns and material of No 3 Section.	
		9pm	2/Lieut Robinson & 13 ORs to relieve 2/Lieut BAILEY	
			2/Lieut BASELOW & 12 ORs " " 2/Lieut WATSON	
			CAPTAIN SPRINGFIELD visited a/a positions	
			1 OR to Hospital	
	16	2am	Carrying party of 20 ORs returned.	
		4am	CAPTAIN SPRINGFIELD, 2/Lieuts BAILEY and WATSON with No 4 Section returned.	
		9am	Working party of NCO & 12 ORs reported to Town Major for fatigue.	
		8.30pm	2/Lieuts IBBERSON and 19 ORs went up line to relieve 2/Lieut BLEAKLEY.	
			CAPTAIN SPRINGFIELD went up to a/a positions.	
			CORPORAL SEAMAN and 4 ORs went up line to relieve CORPL KETTLE.	
			1 OR to Hospital	
			7 ORs reinforcements.	
	17	2.30am	2/Lieut BLEAKLEY and 25 ORs returned.	
		3am	Capt. SPRINGFIELD returned to camp.	
			CORPL KETTLE & 4 ORs returned.	
	18	3pm	Report received from 2/Lieut IBBERSON that one of his guns had been damaged by shell fire.	

WAR DIARY or INTELLIGENCE SUMMARY.

Army Form C. 2118.

(Erase heading not required.)

Place	Date	Hour	Summary of Events and Information	Remarks and references to Appendices
BEHAGNIES	18	8.30 p.m.	2/Lieut SARGENT and 17 O.Rs. went up line at MORT HOMME to relieve 4 guns of 22 M.G. Coy.	
		9.30 p.m.	CAPT. SPRINGFIELD went up line also to visit guns. 2 O.Rs Reinforcements.	
	19	3 p.m.	CAPT. SPRINGFIELD visited all guns. 1 OR Hospital	
	20	3.30 a.m.	" " returned.	
		3 p.m.	2/Lieut BAILEY went up line to see 2/Lieut IBBERSONS positions. Instructions given 2/Lieuts. BAILEY, SARGENT and IBBERSON with regard to proposed raid by 22nd BRIGADE on night of 21st-22nd & machine gun barrage.	
		8.30 p.m.	25 ORs & 3 guns of No 4 Section went up to Mr BAILEY & there relieved 2/Lieut IBBERSONS teams who then got into positions in railway cutting.	
		9.30 p.m.	2/Lieut SARGENT with 17 ORs (4 guns & teams) relieved by 20 M.G. Coy and then got into position in railway cutting N.W. of ECOUST.	
	21		Information received that raid had been postponed until night of 22/23.	
		5.30 p.m.	CAPT. SPRINGFIELD visited 2/Lieut BASELOWS guns returned 8 p.m. 1 OR to Hospital	
	22	1 p.m.	2/Lieuts BLEAKLEY & WATSON went up to 2/Lieuts SARGENT & IBBERSON respectively to help with barrage.	

WAR DIARY or INTELLIGENCE SUMMARY.

Army Form C. 2118.

(Erase heading not required.)

Place	Date	Hour	Summary of Events and Information	Remarks and references to Appendices
BEHAGNIES	22	6 p.m.	Captain SPRINGFIELD went up the line.	
	23		1 OR left Company.	
			Barrage fired	
		5 a.m.	Captain SPRINGFIELD, 2/Lieuts. SARGENT & BLEAKLEY with No. 2 Section and 2/Lieuts. IBBERSON and WATSON with No. 1 Section returned to Camp.	
		8.30 p.m.	2/Lieut. SARGENT & 25 ORs went up line to relieve 2/Lt. ROBINSON & his two teams, & 2/Lt. BASELOW'S two teams. 1 OR. to Hospital	
	24	1 a.m.	2/Lieut. ROBINSON & 25 ORs. returned to Camp.	
			Erection of new camp at MORY Commenced.	
			2/Lieut ROBINSON to hospital sick.	
MORY	25	6.15 a.m.	Coy. HEAD QUARTERS moved to MORY.	
			2 Guns left at BEHAGNIES on a/a duty under 2/Lieut WATSON.	
		5.30 p.m.	2/Lieut IBBERSON went up line to relieve 2/Lieut BASELOW.	
			CAPTAIN SPRINGFIELD visited a/a position up the line.	

WAR DIARY
or
INTELLIGENCE SUMMARY.
(Erase heading not required.)

Army Form C. 2118.

Place	Date	Hour	Summary of Events and Information	Remarks and references to Appendices
MORY	25	8.30 p.m.	2/Lieut BASELOW returned to Camp. 2/Lt BLEAKLEY & 1 OR to VI Corps School	
		9 p.m.	Captain SPRINGFIELD " " ".	
	26		1 officer went on leave to AMIENS. Captain SPRINGFIELD went up line 9 p.m. Work in new camp. 1 OR reinforcement. 1 OR from Hospital 1 OR to Hospital	
	27	4 a.m.	Captain SPRINGFIELD returned from line.	
		5 p.m.	2/Lieut BASELOW went up line to 2/Lt. BAILEY'S gun positions	
		9 p.m.	No. 3 Section went up line to relieve No. 4 Section. 1 OR to Hospital One Officer from leave	
	28	2 a.m.	2/Lieut. BAILEY and 25 ORs of No. 4 Section returned to camp 1 OR to Hospital 2 ORs to U.K. on leave	
		8 p.m.	Capt Springfield went up line	
	29	8 a.m.	" " returned	
	30	4 a.m.	" " went up line - returned 8 a.m.	
		9 p.m.	2/Lt Bailey & 4 guns & teams went up to Mort Homme line to relieve Section of No. 20 M. G. Coy. 2 ORs to Hospital	Fatigue party of 8 ORs to Town Major Fatigues

WAR DIARY
or
INTELLIGENCE SUMMARY.

Army Form C. 2118.

Place	Date	Hour	Summary of Events and Information	Remarks and references to Appendices
MORY	31		Fatigue party of 8 O.Rs. to Town Major Sapignie.	
		8 pm	Captain SPRINGFIELD went up line to visit all guns	
			1 O.R. to Hospital	

F.O. Springfield Capt
for Major.
O.C. 220 M.G. Coy

220 M.G. COY.

WAR DIARY

August 1914.

7th Div:

WAR DIARY
or
INTELLIGENCE SUMMARY.
(Erase heading not required.)

Army Form C. 2118.

220 M G Coy
AUGUST 1917
Vol 6

Place	Date	Hour	Summary of Events and Information	Remarks and references to Appendices
MORY	1	4.30 a.m.	Captain SPRINGFIELD returned to camp from leave	
		11.30 a.m.	2/Lieut IBBERSON came to camp to arrange relief of two gun teams	
		4 p.m.	No 22 M.G. Coy. relieved two guns on A/a duty at BEHAGNIES	
		8.30 p.m.	2/Lieut IBBERSON and 2/Lieut WATSON and 22 ORs went up to Battery A/a positions to relieve No 2 Section	
		11.30 p.m.	2/Lieut SARGENT and 4 gun teams of No 2 Section returned to camp. 2 ORs to Hospital. 1 OR leave to U.K. 1 OR to Sanitary Course	
	2	#	Work in camp - water horse lines etc proceeded with	
		11.30 a.m.	2/Lieut BAILEY and 18 ORs of No 4 Section returned to camp having been relieved by No 22 M.G. Coy.	
	3	4 p.m.	2/Lieut SARGENT went up line to arrange section relief with 2/Lieut BASELOW.	
		8.30 p.m.	22 ORs of No 2 Section went up line to relieve No 3 Section	
		4 p.m.	2/Lieut BAILEY with 2 gun teams relieved No 22 M.G. Coy. on A/a duty at BEHAGNIES.	

WAR DIARY
or
INTELLIGENCE SUMMARY.

(Erase heading not required.)

Army Form C. 2118.

Instructions regarding War Diaries and Intelligence Summaries are contained in F. S. Regs., Part II, and the Staff Manual respectively. Title pages will be prepared in manuscript.

Place	Date	Hour	Summary of Events and Information	Remarks and references to Appendices
MORY	4	7am	2/Lieut BASELOW and 4 teams of No 3 Section returned to Camp	
	5		Work in camp proceeded with. Reports received from 2/Lts Ibberson and Brett regarding destruction by M.G. fire of an enemy aeroplane	
	6	11am	Captain SPRINGFIELD went to view site of new Camp at RANSART	
		6pm	" " " returned	
			Two gun teams of No 2 Section returned to Camp having been relieved by 237 M.G. Coy.	
		4pm	2/Lieut BASELOW & 2 teams of No 3 Section relieved Mr BAILEY & teams on a/a duty at BEHAGNIES. 2/Lieut BAILEY & two teams of No 4 Section returned to camp.	
			1 OR from Sanitary Course.	
			3 ORs leave to U.K	
	7	7am	Captain SPRINGFIELD and Lieut BRETT and advanced party of 4 ORs went to RANSART.	
		5.30pm	Captain SPRINGFIELD & Lieut BRETT returned to camp.	

WAR DIARY or INTELLIGENCE SUMMARY.

Army Form C. 2118.

(Erase heading not required.)

Instructions regarding War Diaries and Intelligence Summaries are contained in F. S. Regs., Part II. and the Staff Manual respectively. Title pages will be prepared in manuscript.

Place	Date	Hour	Summary of Events and Information	Remarks and references to Appendices
MORY	7	4 p.m.	2/Lieut. SARGENT and 2 gunteams of No 2 Section returned to camp having been relieved by 64 M.G. Coy.	
	8		Work of removing material for new camp. 1 OR from Hospital.	
	9	10 a.m.	Two motor lorries loaded left camp with Captain SPRINGFIELD for RANSART.	
		7 p.m.	2/Lieut. Ibbeson returned to camp.	
		11 p.m.	2/Lieut. WATSON & 22 ORs of No 1 Section returned to camp having withdrawn from A/A Battery positions	
		9 p.m.	2/Lieut. BASELOW returned to camp from BEHAGNIES having withdrawn his 2 A/A guns. 1 OR to Hospital. 2 ORs reinforcements from 125 & 126 M.G. Coys. 1 Officer & 2 ORs leave to U.K.	
RANSART	10	8.30 a.m.	Company moved to RANSART. Arrived 3.30 p.m.	
	11		Work in new camp. 4 ORs from U.K. leave. 1 OR from Hospital.	
	12		1 OR from Hospital.	
	13		Work as per programme.	

WAR DIARY or INTELLIGENCE SUMMARY.

Army Form C. 2118.

(Erase heading not required.)

Instructions regarding War Diaries and Intelligence Summaries are contained in F. S. Regs., Part II. and the Staff Manual respectively. Title pages will be prepared in manuscript.

Place	Date	Hour	Summary of Events and Information	Remarks and references to Appendices
RANSART	13		1 OR. to Hospital.	
	14		Work as per programme.	
			1 OR from Leave	
			4 ORs reinforcements.	
	15		Work as per programme	
			1 OR from Hospital	
			1 OR. reinforcement	
	16		Work as per programme. 1 OR to Hospital. 1 OR from Hospital	
			1 OR. reinforcement.	
	17		Work as per programme. 2 ORs to Hospital 1 OR from Hospital	
	18		" " " " 1 OR to " 1 OR " "	
	19		3 ORs from leave to U.K.	
	20		Work as per programme (firing on range)	
		4 p.m.	Major Matheson & Capt. Springfield went to Divisional Conference	
			2 ORs to Hospital.	

WAR DIARY or INTELLIGENCE SUMMARY.

Army Form C. 2118.

(Erase heading not required.)

Place	Date	Hour	Summary of Events and Information	Remarks and references to Appendices
RANSART	21		Work as per programme.	
			C.Q.M.S. Wright joined Coy as C.S.M. (Warrant Officer Class II) from 91 M.G. Coy.	
	22		Work as per programme.	
		7 p.m.	Lieut BRETT from U.K. leave. 1 O.R. from U.K. leave.	
		8.30 p.m.	O.C. & 1 O.R. leave on duty to BASE to see Coy. records.	
			4 O.Rs reinforcements. 1 O.R. to Hospital. 1 O.R. from Hospital	
	23		Work as per programme.	
		7 p.m.	2/Lt. BLEAKLEY and 1 O.R. from VI Corps School.	
	24	8.30 a.m.	Coy. left camp under 2/Lieut. SARGENT to proceed to demonstration of attack by 22nd Inf Brigade. Returned 5.45 p.m.	
	25		DIVISIONAL FAIR.	
		10 p.m.	D.M.G.O. on leave to U.K.	
	26	7 p.m.	O.C. & 1 O.R. from BASE.	
	27	11.30 a.m.	2/Lieut BASELOW went to PAS.	
		5 p.m.	2/Lieut BLEAKLEY and 2 ORs to DOULLENS for billeting purposes.	

WAR DIARY or INTELLIGENCE SUMMARY.

Army Form C. 2118.

Place	Date	Hour	Summary of Events and Information	Remarks and references to Appendices
RANSART	27	4.30 p.m.	2/Lieut IBBERSON & 4 N.C.Os. to lecture on bayonet fighting at GROSVILLE.	
			Work in Camp preparing for move.	
			2 ORs to Hospital. 1 OR to base (inefficient). 1 OR to TANK CORPS on probation.	
		6 p.m.	2/Lieut BAILEY on leave to U.K.	
	28	9 a.m.	Company under O.C. marched to PAS EN ARTOIS. arrived 2.30 p.m.	
			2/Lieut BASELOW rejoined Coy.	
PAS EN ARTOIS	29	10.30 a.m.	OCs inspection of Company.	
	30	2.30 a.m.	TRANSPORT and N° 2 Section with Lieuts. DURRANT and BRETT & 2/Lieut SARGENT marched to MONDICOURT for entraining.	
		4 a.m.	Remainder of Coy. under O.C. marched to MONDICOURT.	
		6.31 a.m.	TRAIN left MONDICOURT.	
		3 p.m.	Detrained at HOPOUTRE and marched to HEYMANS FARM, BEAUVOORDE.	
BEAUVOORDE	31		Parades and inspections in Camp.	
			1 O.R. from Hospital. 1 O.R. reinforcement.	

WAR DIARY
or
INTELLIGENCE SUMMARY.

(Erase heading not required.)

Army Form C. 2118.

Place	Date	Hour	Summary of Events and Information	Remarks and references to Appendices
BEAUVOORDE	31	4 p.m.	2/Lieut IBBERSON with 2 gun teams left camp to mount 2 guns in the vicinity of Divisional H.Q. RENINGHELST for a/a purposes.	

E.D. Springfield
Capt
O.C. 220 M.G. Coy

WAR DIARY

220
M. G. COY.
September 1914.

7th Div:

WAR DIARY
or
INTELLIGENCE SUMMARY.
(Erase heading not required.)

220 M.G. Coy
Army Form C. 2118.

SEPTEMBER

Vol 7

Place	Date	Hour	Summary of Events and Information	Remarks and references to Appendices
BEAUVOORDE	1		Parades in Camp.	
		9.am	2/Lieut BLEAKLEY and 3 ORs to Corps reinforcement Camp for purposes of instructing.	
			C.S.M. WRIGHT leave to UK.	
	2	1pm	2/Lieut BLEAKLEY and 3 ORs returned to Camp.	
	3	5pm	2/Lieut IBBERSON and 2 gun teams went to HAZEBROUCK with Division for a/a duty	
			1 OR leave to UK. 1 OR to Hospital.	
	4	2pm	Company under O.C. marched to HAZEBROUCK. Arrived at 6.30 pm.	
HAZEBROUCK	5		2/Lieut ROBINSON mounted 2 guns of No 3 Section for a/a duty	
			2/Lieut SARGENT " 2 " of No 2 " " "	
			Major Matheson from leave.	
			1 OR leave to UK. 2 ORs to Hospital	
	6		2/Lieut BASELOW mounted 2 guns of No 4 Section for a/a duty	
			2 ORs reinforcements	
	8		2/Lieut BLEAKLEY relieved 2/Lieut Sargent in a/a positions.	

WAR DIARY or INTELLIGENCE SUMMARY.

Army Form C. 2118.

Instructions regarding War Diaries and Intelligence Summaries are contained in F. S. Regs., Part II. and the Staff Manual respectively. Title pages will be prepared in manuscript.

(Erase heading not required.)

Place	Date	Hour	Summary of Events and Information	Remarks and references to Appendices
HAZEBROUCK	8		1 Officer on UK leave (2/Lt IBBERSON) 1 OR from leave.	
	9		2/Lieut BAILEY from leave to UK. 1 OR to Hospital	
	10		Captain SPRINGFIELD on leave to UK. 1 N.C.O. to Divisional Gas School Course.	
	11		1 OR to Hospital	
	12		1 OR from Hospital	
	13	11·00 a.m.	Company under Lieut DURRANT marched to ARQUES. Arrived 5.30 p.m. D.M.G.O. & 2/Lieuts WATSON, BLEAKLEY, ROBINSON & BAILEY with 8 a/a guns and teams remained at HAZEBROUCK	
ARQUES	14		2 ORs from leave to U.K. 1 OR to Hospital 1 OR from Hospital	
	15	8.30 a.m.	Company under LIEUT DURRANT marched to WESTBECOURT. Arrived at 2·0 p.m. 1 OR to Hospital 1 OR on leave to UK	

WAR DIARY
or
INTELLIGENCE SUMMARY.
(Erase heading not required.)

Army Form C. 2118.

Place	Date	Hour	Summary of Events and Information	Remarks and references to Appendices
WESTBECOURT	16	1.30 p.m.	D.M.G.O. & 4 subsections rejoined Company from HAZEBROUCK. 1 N.C.O. from Divisional Gas Course	
	17		2/Lieut SARGENT on leave to U.K. 2 ORs from UK leave. 2 ORs to Hospital.	
	18		Work (training in ACQUIN district) as per programme. 1 OR to Hospital.	
	19		Work as per programme. 1 OR on leave to UK. 1 OR to Hospital. 1 OR Reinforcement	
	20		1 OR to Hospital. Work as per programme.	
	21		2/Lieut IBBERSON from UK leave. Work as per programme. 1 OR to Hospital	
	22		O.C. from Leave to U.K. Firing on Range. 1 OR on leave to U.K.	

WAR DIARY
or
INTELLIGENCE SUMMARY.

(Erase heading not required.)

Army Form C. 2118.

Instructions regarding War Diaries and Intelligence Summaries are contained in F. S. Regs., Part II. and the Staff Manual respectively. Title pages will be prepared in manuscript.

Place	Date	Hour	Summary of Events and Information	Remarks and references to Appendices
WESTBECOURT	23		1 OR. to Hospital.	
	24	8.15 a.m.	Divisional Practice Attack. Returned 6 p.m.	
			1 OR to Hospital. 1 OR UK leave. 1 OR from UK leave.	
			2 ORs returned to base inefficient.	
	25	8.15 a.m.	Divisional Practice attack. Returned 5.15 p.m.	
			1 OR to Hospital.	
	26	8.15 a.m.	Divisional Practice attack. Returned 5 p.m.	
			2 ORs to Hospital.	
	27	2.30 p.m.	Company under O.C. marched to WIZERNES. arrived 6 p.m.	
			1 OR on leave to U.K.	
WIZERNES	28	2.15 p.m.	Transport with Lt BRETT & 2/Lt BASELOW moved to STAPLE area, with 54 ORs	
	29	8.30	Coy. moved by lorries from WIZERNES to CHATEAU SEGARD. Arrived 1 p.m.	
		4 p.m.	Received orders for Coy. to go back to WESTOUTRE. Arrived 5.30 p.m. & rejoined transport	
WESTOUTRE	30	4 a.m.	DMGO & O.C. reconnoitred line.	
		10 a.m.	Coy. under 2nd in Command moved to CHATEAU SEGARD. arrived 1 p.m.	
			2 ORs transferred to 207 M.G. Coy. 1 OR from UK leave	
			2 ORs to CAMIERS M.G. Course. (Sergeants WRIGHT & MORRISON)	

WAR DIARY
or
INTELLIGENCE SUMMARY.
(Erase heading not required.)

Instructions regarding War Diaries and Intelligence Summaries are contained in F. S. Regs., Part II. and the Staff Manual respectively. Title pages will be prepared in manuscript.

Army Form C. 21

Place	Date	Hour	Summary of Events and Information	Remarks and references to Appendices
CHATEAU SEGARD	30		2/Lieut SARGENT from U.K. leave. Work in new camp.	

B Durrant Lieut
for OC 220 M.G. Coy

WAR DIARY

220 M.G. COY.

October 1914.

7th Div:

WAR DIARY
or
INTELLIGENCE SUMMARY.
(Erase heading not required.)

220 M.G. Coy
Army Form C. 2118.
OCTOBER 1917.
Vol 8

Place	Date	Hour	Summary of Events and Information	Remarks and references to Appendices
CHATEAU SEGARD	1	10am	O.C. started to reconnoitre the line with all Officers. On reaching GLENCORSE WOOD reconnaissance greatly hindered by hostile barrage. It was determined to reconnoitre again the following morning and all officers returned to Camp at 5.0 p.m. 2/Lieut BLEAKLEY on leave to U.K. 1 O.R. to Hospital. 1 O.R. from Hospital.	
		9pm	2/Lieut IBBERSON went to HOOGE CRATER to meet a carrying party of 250 O.Rs from H.A.C. to carry S.A.A. from HOOGE to the BUTTE in POLYGON WOOD. 80000 rounds were taken up and the dump formed. 2/Lt IBBERSON returned to Camp 4 a.m. 2/10/17	
		10pm	O.C. and Transport Officer left Camp with pack train of 32 animals including 8 supplied by 91 M.G.Coy. & took 64000 rounds from HOOGE to N.W. Corner of POLYGON WOOD. 1 animal killed 1 wounded O.C. remained at HOOGE and was met by all Section officers at 6am 4/10/17. Thorough reconnaissance made and battery	

WAR DIARY or INTELLIGENCE SUMMARY.

Army Form C. 2118.

(Erase heading not required.)

Place	Date	Hour	Summary of Events and Information	Remarks and references to Appendices
			positions and Coy. H.Q chosen. All officers returned to Camp at 10 a.m. 2/10/17. 1 O.R. to UK Officers Cadet School (Pte Richards G)	
	2	3 pm	2/Lieut SARGENT reconnoitred line of march from Camp to HOOGE CRATER on the 2/10/17. O.R.s from UK draft. 3 O.Rs reinforcements	
		6 pm	2/Lieut IBBERSON went to HOOGE CRATER to meet carrying party of 100 O.Rs RAC to carry SAA from GILLMORE'S Road to forward dump. Party had been delayed and did not arrive til 12 midnight. 2/Lieut IBBERSON returned at 7.30 a.m. 3/10/17	
		9 pm	2 officers and carrying party of 60 O.Rs reported to Lieut BAKER 2n M.G Coy. to carry forward SAA to new dump. Number of rounds taken up 80000. This party returned to Camp at 3.0 a.m.	
	3	2 pm	Lt BRETT (Transport Officer) took all fighting limbers and gun stores to HOOGE CRATERS & formed Company dump. Returned to camp at 4 p.m.	

WAR DIARY
or
INTELLIGENCE SUMMARY.
(Erase heading not required.)

Place	Date	Hour	Summary of Events and Information	Remarks and references to Appendices
CHATEAU SEGARD	3	4pm to 6pm	Vicinity of camp shelled by long range hostile guns. All shells with one exception blind. No casualties sustained.	
		5.30 pm	Carrying party of 50 ohs from R Warwickshire Regt reported and 3 men per gun team told off as ammunition carriers	
		6pm	Company under O.C. left camp and marched to HOOGE CRATER via Zillebeke. Guns &c. manhandled to battery positions N.W. corner of POLYGON WOOD. Enemy shelling very light. All guns in position by 12 midnight. Casualties 2 ohs killed.	
	4	5.30 a.m.	Hostile barrage put down forward of battery position. No casualties. 6 a.m. Barrage put down as per arranged scheme. All guns fired.	
		6.30	Company moved forward to take up new battery positions. Hostile shelling light. 2 ohs wounded during move forward.	
		8 a.m.	14 out of 16 guns ready for action. Two gun teams delayed owing to casualties. Hostile shelling increasing	

WAR DIARY or INTELLIGENCE SUMMARY

Army Form C. 2118.

Place	Date	Hour	Summary of Events and Information	Remarks and references to Appendices
CHATEAU SEGARD	4	8.30 am	14 guns organised on S.O.S. lines. Hostile shelling heavy. Several casualties in gun teams. 2 guns out of action. Coy. artificers wounded at Coy. H.Q. situated at the BUTTE, POLYGON WOOD, and guns unable to be repaired.	
		9 am	Lieut BRETT arrived at Coy H.Q. with 10 pack animals carrying remaining gun stores and water. Intermittent shelling till 1.0 p.m. when S.O.S. signal sent up. Guns fired at pre-arranged rate for 20 minutes.	
		5.30 pm	2/Lieut. IBBERSON arrived with rations on pack animals.	
		6 pm	S.O.S. again sent up. Some rain having fallen belts were inclined to be damp and some difficulty was experienced. During night harassing fire was maintained & S.O.S. lines fired on when called for. Casualties to 6 p.m. O.R. 3 killed 18 wounded (2 slightly - at duty). During the day 10 pack animals joined part of Divisional M.G. train under Lieut. BAKER, 20 M.G. Coy & brought forward SAA water etc to the BUTTE.	

WAR DIARY or INTELLIGENCE SUMMARY.

Army Form C. 2118.

Place	Date	Hour	Summary of Events and Information	Remarks and references to Appendices
CHATEAU SEGARD	5	8 am	Owing to casualties 12 gun teams only could be formed and S.O.S. line was altered accordingly.	
		9.30 am	D.M.G.O. visited Company H.Q. and all Coy. guns in position.	
			O.C. & 2/Lt BASELOW went down to HOOGE to organise Coy. dump there.	
		11 am	S.O.S. called for and fire maintained for 20 minutes.	
		12.0 noon	O.C. & 2/Lt BASELOW returned to Coy H.Q.	
		5 pm	Direct hit on Coy. H.Q. killing 2/Lieuts SARGENT, IBBERSON and BASELOW, and severely wounding C.S.M. WRIGHT.	
		6 pm	Rations arrived on pack animals.	
		7 pm	Counter attack developed & S.O.S. barrage put down. Enemy shelling during the day light. Weather fine with some rain. Casualties to 6 pm. Officers 3 killed, ORs 1 killed 3 wounded.	
		11 pm	SOS barrage fired.	
	6	1 am	SOS barrage fired.	
		11 am	O.C. & 2/Lt ROBINSON went to HOOGE to ascertain situation.	
		12 noon	Orders received for Company to be withdrawn.	

WAR DIARY or INTELLIGENCE SUMMARY.

Army Form C. 2118.

(Erase heading not required.)

Place	Date	Hour	Summary of Events and Information	Remarks and references to Appendices
CHATEAU SEGARD	6	5pm	Company returned to Camp, gun stores being brought from HOOGE CRATER by limber. 8 pack animals under Lt BRETT brought back 8 guns & tripods. Casualties to 6pm ORs 1 killed 4 wounded. In spite of bad weather conditions and fairly heavy hostile shelling no difficulty was experienced in keeping up supplies of ammunition, gun stores, rations etc. Pack animals proved very useful & saved man-handling heavy stores long distances.	
	7		1 OR to Hospital. 1 OR slightly wounded remained at duty. Orders received that eight guns of 220 M.G. Coy would relieve 8 guns of the 91st M.G. Coy on barrage lines & would assist by barrages a minor operation to be carried out on the morning of the 9th. 1 OR to Hospital.	
	8	2pm	8 gun teams with guns on pack animals left camp under O.C.	

WAR DIARY or **INTELLIGENCE SUMMARY.**

Army Form C. 2118.

(Erase heading not required.)

Place	Date	Hour	Summary of Events and Information	Remarks and references to Appendices
CHATEAU SEGARD	8		Pack mules off-loaded at HOOGE CRATERS and gun stuff man-handled to the BUTTE, POLYGON WOOD.	
		5pm	91st M.G. Coy were relieved	
			During the night the battery positions were heavily shelled and heavy rain fell.	
			1 O.R. leave to U.K.	
	9	9am	Barrages put down in accordance with scheme and guns remained on S.O.S. lines.	
		5.15 pm	S.O.S. signal went up on left of Divisional front. Guns answered with short barrage. One gun put out of action by shell fire.	
			Casualties to 6 pm O.R.s 4 wounded	
		2 p.m	Ration party of 18 o.r.s under Corporal SIMS and with 2 limbers as far as YPRES carried up to gun positions – 1 o.r. wounded.	
			Information received regarding Divisional relief	
	10		Quiet day. BUTTE enfiladed by shell fire from the right.	

WAR DIARY or INTELLIGENCE SUMMARY.

(Erase heading not required.)

Army Form C. 2118.

Place	Date	Hour	Summary of Events and Information	Remarks and references to Appendices
CHATEAU SEGARD	10	3 p.m.	Orders from D.M.G.O. received by O.C. that 2 guns would relieve 2 guns of 110 Coy M.G.C. in JETTY WOOD, 2 guns to relieve 2 guns of 110 M G Coy on the right of REUTEL, 2 guns to move forward to JOLTING HOUSES and 2 guns to remain at BATTERY positions. Owing to the dark night and the guides provided losing their way, only the guns at JETTY WOOD had reached their positions by daybreak. CASUALTIES to 6 p.m. 2 ORs wounded. Information received that 220 M.G. Coy's guns would be relieved night of 11/12 by 68 and 70 M.G. Coys. 1 O.R. to Hospital (sick).	
		2.15 p.m.	Ration party under Corporal COOMBS went up with rations.	
	11		O.C's 68 and 70 M. G. Coys. went to advanced Coy. H. Q. and arranged relief and withdrawal of all guns of this Company for that evening. All guns either withdrawn or relieved by 5.30 p.m. Casualties to 6 p.m. ORs 1 wounded	

WAR DIARY
or
INTELLIGENCE SUMMARY.
(Erase heading not required.)

Army Form C. 2118.

Instructions regarding War Diaries and Intelligence Summaries are contained in F. S. Regs., Part II. and the Staff Manual respectively. Title pages will be prepared in manuscript.

Place	Date	Hour	Summary of Events and Information	Remarks and references to Appendices
CHATEAU SEGARD	11	7pm	Company returned to Camp. 1 O.R. leave to U.K.	
	12		1 O.R. from leave to U.K. 2/Lieuts. COSTAIN, MARSHALL and GILBERT reinforcements	
			D.M.G.O. attached to Divisional H.Q. with servant and groom.	
		3pm	Company under O.C. marched to ZEVECOTEN arrived 5.30 p.m.	
ZEVECOTEN	13		2/Lieut. BLEAKLEY from UK leave	
			50 O.R. reinforcements. 1 OR to Hospital	
	14		Inspection parades & clothing etc parades	
	15		Arms, gun and barrage drill in vicinity of Camp.	
			1 OR leave to U.K.	
	16		Drill in vicinity of Camp	
			Corporal MILES to BASE DEPOT for COURSE at GRANTHAM.	
	17		Drill in vicinity of Camp	
			1 O.R. from leave	
	18		Work in vicinity of camp. 1 OR leave to UK	

WAR DIARY or INTELLIGENCE SUMMARY

Army Form C. 2118.

(Erase heading not required.)

Place	Date	Hour	Summary of Events and Information	Remarks and references to Appendices
ZEVECOTEN	19	4 a.m.	OC and LIEUT BRETT reconnoitred line (new 7th Divisional area). returned at 12 noon. 3 ORs to Hospital.	
		2 p.m.	Company marched to CAMP 50 (midway between RENINGHELST and BOESCHEPE).	
CAMP 50 (WESTOUTRE AREA)	20		Parades in vicinity of Camp.	
		10 a.m.	OC went to Divisional H.Q. returned 4 p.m. having made arrangements for forming ammunition dump for barrage in connection with forthcoming attack by Division.	✗
	21	9.15 a.m.	LIEUT. BRETT & 2/Lieut. COSTAIN with 22 ORs and 12 pack mules left Camp to proceed to VOORMEZEELE to form pack train as per attached instructions	
		11 a.m.	OC's inspection of Company. 1 OR from Hospital. 1 OR reinforcement.	
	22	1 a.m.	2/Lieut COSTAIN went to BARDENBURG with 16 pack animals to obtain S.A.A. Rejoined pack train & proceeded up line at 5 a.m. under Lieut BRETT with 48 pack animals + leaders with 6 ORs loaders. S.A.A. handed over to carrying party of 39th DIVISION. Pack train returned to VOORMEZEELE at 9 a.m.	
		10 a.m.	OC went to DIVISIONAL H.Q to arrange barrage programme in conjunction with proposed attack by 7th Division.	

WAR DIARY
or
INTELLIGENCE SUMMARY.
(Erase heading not required.)

Army Form C. 2118.

Place	Date	Hour	Summary of Events and Information	Remarks and references to Appendices
CAMP 50 (WESTOUTRE AREA)	22		2/Lieut. ROBINSON on leave to U.K. 1 OR from U.K. leave. 1 OR from Hospital. 1 OR to Hospital.	
	23	4.45 a.m.	Lieut BRETT and 2/Lieut. COSTAIN took S.A.A. up line with pack animals. Returned 9.30 a.m. 1 pack animal killed.	
		10 a.m.	LIEUT DURRANT went to VOORMEZEELE and LOCK 8 to reconnoitre new camp and dug-outs. Returned 5 p.m.	
		2 p.m.	O.C. went to DIVISIONAL H.Q. to make further arrangements for attack. 1 O.R. from Hospital.	
	24	4.30 a.m.	Lieut. BRETT and 2/Lieut. COSTAIN took S.A.A. up line with pack animals. Returned 9.0 a.m.	
		12.0 noon	Company under O.C. marched to LOCK 8 (YPRES-COMMINES CANAL) and stayed night in dug-outs.	
		10 a.m.	2/Lieut. BAILEY with 4 ammunition limbers and 9 ORs proceeded to CHEAPSIDE to form rear Company H.Q. Remainder of transport joined LIEUT BRETT at VOORMEZEELE. 1 OR to Hospital.	

WAR DIARY or INTELLIGENCE SUMMARY

Place	Date	Hour	Summary of Events and Information	Remarks and references to Appendices
LOCK 8	25	4 a.m.	Carrying party of 64 ORs. under O.C. with Section Officers went up line with ammunition in belt boxes to form dump at gun positions and returned 8 a.m. Casualties 2 ORs killed.	
		4.30 a.m.	Lieut. BRETT and 2/Lieut. COSTAIN took S.A.A. up line with pack animals. Returned at 9.30 a.m.	
		4 p.m.	Company by Sections under Section Officers (+74 ORs) went up line with a carrying party in addition of 16 ORs and 18 pack mules. These 16 ORs returned to camp at midnight.	
		4.30 p.m.	O.C. and D.M.O.C. went up line.	
		5 p.m.	Forward Coy. H.Q. and details joined Lieut. BRETT at VOORMEZEELE. 1 OR leave to U.K. All guns in position by 6 p.m. Casualties NIL. Enemy shelling during the night slight. Rain fell heavily making the ground well nigh impassable.	
	26	5.40 a.m.	Attack started and barrage put down by 16 guns plus 4 guns of No. 20 M.G. Coy forming one group under O.C. Great difficulty experienced in keeping guns in action owing to enemy shelling	

Place	Date	Hour	Summary of Events and Information	Remarks and references to Appendices
	26 (contd)		throwing large quantities of mud on the guns.	
		8.15 a.m.	Guns taken down in rotation and cleaned - this proved very difficult owing to rain falling at the time and absence of cover. Two guns found to be temporarily out of action. During the day enemy continued to shell M.G. battery area heavily and by 8 p.m. 3 more guns were out of action and two teams had been buried by shell fire but had been dugout. Casualties 3 killed and 1 wounded O.Rs.	
	27	6.45 a.m.	2/Lieut COSTAIN left camp at VOORMEZEELE with 30 ORs to carry S.A.A. from CLONMEL COPSE to gun positions. All returned by 10 a.m.	
		8.15 a.m.	Damaged guns and teams under OC withdrawn to HEDGES STREET dugouts. Teams reorganised and four teams sent forward under 2/Lieut MARSHALL to relieve No. 116 M.G. Coy. on battery positions in CLONMEL COPSE. Relief complete by 10.30 a.m.	
		1 p.m.	Party of 19 ORs and 5 pack animals left camp under Lieut. BRETT	

WAR DIARY
or
INTELLIGENCE SUMMARY.
(Erase heading not required.)

Army Form C. 2118.

Instructions regarding War Diaries and Intelligence Summaries are contained in F. S. Regs., Part II. and the Staff Manual respectively. Title pages will be prepared in manuscript.

Place	Date	Hour	Summary of Events and Information	Remarks and references to Appendices
	27 (cont)		with rations. Returned 5 p.m. Casualties O.Rs. 1 killed 7 wounded.	
	26	4.30 p.m.	Enemy reported concentrating at SWAGGER FARM on guns concentrated and switched accordingly & fire opened.	
		5 p.m.	S.O.S. sent up to the left but no attack developed from the direction of SWAGGER FARM.	
	27	1 a.m.	Orders received from D.M.G.O. that all available guns should be laid on new S.O.S. lines N. of the YPRES-MENIN ROAD.	
	28		Situation normal. Information received that Company would be relieved on morning of the 29th. D.M.G.O's instructions attached.	
	29		Withdrawal of 6 guns as mentioned in M/100 completed by 8 a.m.	(M/100 destroyed in error & copy unobtainable in time)
		11 a.m.	4 guns in CLONMEL COPSE relieved by 228 M.G.Coy.	
		4 p.m.	All men & stores collected at VOORMEZEELE CAMP. 1 OR leave to U.K.	
	30	9 a.m.	Transport under Lieut BRETT with 2/Lieut COSTAIN proceeded to new area	

WAR DIARY or INTELLIGENCE SUMMARY.

Army Form C. 2118.

(Erase heading not required.)

Place	Date	Hour	Summary of Events and Information	Remarks and references to Appendices
	30	2 p.m.	Company under O.C. (less TRANSPORT) left VOORMEZEELE and marched to OUDERDOM Railhead. Entrained and arrived at EBLINGHEM at 9 p.m. Marched to BLAIRINGHEM, arrived 10:30 p.m. 2 ORs (Sergeants WRIGHT & MORRISON) from CAMIERS COURSE. 3 ORs from leave to U.K. 1 OR to Hospital (gassed). 2 ORs from Hospital. 6 ORs reinforcements.	
BLAIRINGHEM	31	12 noon	TRANSPORT under Lieut BRETT and 2/Lieut COSTAIN joined Company having spent the night at HAZEBROUCK. 2/Lieut MARSHALL to C.C.S. (sick).	

L. Young Capt
O.C. 220 L of C Coy

Secret.

20th Infantry Brigade.
22nd   "
91st   "
220th M.G. Company.

1. On the 21st instant a pack train of 48 mules will be formed at VOORMEZEELE and will work under the orders of Lieut. EMPT, 220th M.G. Coy.

2. To form this pack train each M.G. Coy., will detail 12 mules (with loaders) 8 with pack saddles and 4 without, to report to Lieut. EMPT at S.A.A. Dump VOORMEZEELE by 3 p.m. 21st instant.

   Lieut. EMPT will proceed in advance and arrange transport lines.

   He will detail guides to meet the parties from the other 3 M.G. Coys at road junction at I.31.c.3.8. and to conduct them to the transport lines.

3. The pack train will be billeted at VOORMEZEELE, and will remain there until probably the 25th instant.

4. Rations for consumption on the 22nd and 23rd instant should be taken up tomorrow. Each Company will make its own arrangements about rations.

5. Detailed instructions will be given to Lieut. EMPT by O.C. 220th M.G. Company.

6. O.C. 22nd and O.C. 220th M.G. Coys will detail one officer each to assist Lieut. EMPT.

   Separate instructions are being issued by the D.M.G.O. to the officer detailed by O.C. 22nd M.G. Coy.

7. O's.C. 22nd and 220th M.G. Coy. will also detail 6 men each to proceed to VOORMEZEELE. These men will not be loaders.

8. 20 extra pack saddles are being supplied by 39th Division.

October 20th, 1917.

B. Fairy
Lieut-Colonel,
A.A. & Q.M.G., 7th DIVISION.

WAR DIARY

220 M.G. COY.

November 1917.

7th Div:

WAR DIARY or INTELLIGENCE SUMMARY.

220 M.G. Coy

NOVEMBER 1919

Army Form C. 2118.

Place	Date	Hour	Summary of Events and Information	Remarks and references to Appendices
BLARINGHEM	1		Parades in Camp. Taking inventory of stores etc.	
			1 O.R. to Hospital	
	2		Parades in Camp.	
			2/Lieut Marshall evacuated from C.C.S. (Sick)	
			3 O.Rs to Hospital	
	3		Parades in Camp	
			2/Lieut Robinson returned from U.K. leave	
			1 O.R. to Hospital	
			1 O.R. rejoined from C.C.S.	
	4		Church Parades.	
			14 O.R. Reinforcements from Base Depot	
			1 O.R. to Hospital	
			C.S.M. Hiles arrived from 126 P.O.W company as witness for F.G.C.M.	
	5	9.0 AM	Route March	
		2.0 PM	Parades in Camp	
			Sgt Billington arrived from 15 Canadian M.G. Coy. as witness for F.G.C.M.	

WAR DIARY or INTELLIGENCE SUMMARY.

Army Form C. 2118.

(Erase heading not required.)

Place	Date	Hour	Summary of Events and Information	Remarks and references to Appendices
	5	Cont'd	2 O.Rs to Hospital	
			3 O.Rs attached for Rations	
			4 O.R from Hospital	
			1 O.R on Fullerphone Course	
	6	9.0AM	Tactical Scheme	
		2:30PM	Parades in Camp.	
	7		Special Order received that the King of the Belgians would inspect the Division on the 8th	
			Parades. Cleaning for inspection	
			Lieut Durrant leave to U.K	
			2/Lt Bailey + 1 O.R to G.H.Q Small Arms School	
			Sgt Bell arrived from M.G. Base Depot as witness for F.G.C.M	
			Orders received to move on 12th inst to FAUQUEMBERGUES	
			1 O.R reinforcement	
	8	8.30 pm	Inspection by the King of the Belgians	
	9		2/Lieut. Watson leave to U.K.	
	10		1 OR leave to U.K.	

WAR DIARY or INTELLIGENCE SUMMARY.

Army Form C. 2118.

(Erase heading not required.)

Place	Date	Hour	Summary of Events and Information	Remarks and references to Appendices
BLAIRINGHEM	11		C.S.M HILES, Sgt. BILLINGTON & Sgt BEEL returned to their Units on Completion of duty with this Company.	
		11 a.m.	Church Parade.	
			1 o.r. from leave.	
	12	7 a.m.	Company left BLAIRINGHEM and marched to FAUQUEMBERGUES. Arrived at 3 p.m.	I
				vide Attached Orders
			1 o.r. to Hospital. 5 o.rs returned to BASE.	
FAUQUEMBERGUES	13		Cleaning limbers guns etc.	
			2 o.rs to Hospital.	
	14	9 a.m.	Company under O.C. marched to CANLERS. Arrived 3 p.m.	
CANLERS	15		2/Lieut. BAILEY and 1 o.r from M.G. Base School.	
			Lieut. CHEESMAN joined Company as reinforcement.	
			4 o.rs. reinforcements.	
	16		Parades in Camp.	

WAR DIARY or INTELLIGENCE SUMMARY.

Army Form C. 2118.

(Erase heading not required.)

Place	Date	Hour	Summary of Events and Information	Remarks and references to Appendices
CANLERS	17		Attached entraining orders received from 20th Infantry Brigade.	II
		9.30 am	Company marched under O.C. to ECLIMEUX. Arrived at 1.30 p.m. (vide attached orders).	
	18		Parades in Camp.	
	19	1.45 pm	Coy. marched to WAVRANS for entraining. Train left at 8.30 pm. (vide attached orders)	III
			Lieut DURRANT, 2/Lieut. WATSON and 10 OR from leave to U.K.	
			4 ORs reinforcements.	
	20 21 22 23 24 25		In the train.	
	26	9 am	Detrained at LEGNAGO and marched to SABBION	
SABBION	27	1 pm	Company under O.C. marched to SPESSA. Arrived 4 pm.	
	28	9.30 am	" " " " " " VILLAGA " 1.30 pm.	
	29	10.30 am	" " " " " " MONTEGALDELLA 1.30 pm	

WAR DIARY
or
INTELLIGENCE SUMMARY.

Army Form C. 2118.

(Erase heading not required.)

Place	Date	Hour	Summary of Events and Information	Remarks and references to Appendices
VILLAGA	30	10 am	Company under O.C. marched to LISSARO. Arrived 1 p.m.	

Dunant Lieut
for O.C. 220 Machine Gun Coy.

220 Machine Gun Coy
Movement Order No. 2

The Coy will move tomorrow 12th inst. to FAUQUEMBERGUES by march route.

Parade ready to move off 6-40 a.m.

Dress Fighting Order, service caps. Waterbottles full. Steel helmets on haversacks.

Rations Haversack rations for mid-day meal will be carried on the man. Dinners will be served on arrival in new area. Hot tea will be carried in containers on cooks cart for mid-day meal.

Transport The Transport less Cooks cart will march as an independent unit under R.S. Brett. Transport will be clear of billet No. 37 by 7-30 a.m.

Packing Packs & horse rugs will be the only extra articles on fighting limbers. Bulk S.A.A. will be divided out between Ammunition limbers. Ammunition limbers will be loaded as usual with the exception of 4.5. Waggon Load. C.Q.M.S Stores etc. A.3. which is allotted to the transport. Two lorries are allotted to the Coy and will be loaded as under:

No. 1 LORRY   No. 2 LORRY
BLANKETS   MESS STORES
COOKS STORES   OFFICE "
    OFFICERS VALISES
    TENTS.

Lorries L/Cpl Williams will be i/c No. 1 Lorry. Loaders — 2 Cooks — Pa. Jefferies
L/Cpl Bombley will be i/c No. 2 Lorry. Loaders — Ptes Allgar, Champken & White.
Ptes Jefferies & White will be at Camp Commandants Office at 8-15 a.m. as guides for lorries. No. 1 Lorry will be taken to Billet No. 36 & then on to Coy. No. 2 Lorry will be taken to Billet No. 36 & then to Officers Mess & then on to C.B 36. 2/Lt Costain will be i/c Lorries & report to 2/Lt Bleakley in new area.

2.

BLANKETS. Blankets will be rolled, labelled & collected as follows

by 6-0 a.m.
Nos 3+4 Sects.   at No 36.   No 1. & 2 Sects
Transport   at
H.Q. & Servants   No 37

Watercart will march half full.

Cooks Cart will call at Officers Mess at 6-30 a.m. for a box &
then proceed to billet No 37 for food containers.
It will march in rear of Coy.
These will be absolutely clean by 6-30 a.m.

Billets
an N.C.O & one man per Section will be left at
Billets till they have been seen by Section
Officers. Section Officers will report to D.C
that their respective billets are clean by 7-0 am.

Bricksmen These will be detailed by Sections before
          parade & remain at the limbers.
          2/Lt Gilbert is detailed for special duty.

Duty   particulars of which will be given him direct
         by O.C. Coy.

Officers Valises. These will be packed & collected at
         Billet No 36 by 6-30 a.m.

Issued at 4-30 p.m. 11/11/17 to all concerned.

W D Corry   K.C. Springfield. Capt.
                                   O.C. 220 M.G. Coy.

220 MACHINE GUN COMPANY.

Move Order No. 4.

No. 1. The Company will move to ECLIMEUX to-morrow. Parade. 9-30 a.m. ready to move off. Dress-Full marching order. Steel Helmets on packs.

No. 2. Leather Jerkins on fighting limbers. Horse rugs on limbers.

No. 3. Loads.
- A.3. Transport.
- B.3. Signals, Artificer, Lieuts Bleakley & Bailey's valises.
- C.3. Bootmaker, Lieut's Cheesman, Watson, Robinson & Gilbert's valises.
- D.3. Office Stores, Officers Mess Stores.
- G.S. Waggon. CQMS Stores, O.C's, 2nd 1/c, T.O. & 2nd Lieut's Costain's valises.

No. 4. Lorry. One lorry is allotted to the Coy under charge of Lieut. Cheesman. One blanket per man - extra blankets -surplus kits, etc.
Load.
Cooks Cart. Cooks Stores.
Sergt. Sadler, Ptes Smith C, Vinall & Temple will form a guard and go with the above stores on the lorry on its second journey direct to WAVRAN. They will take rations up to the night of the 19th. This lorry will be met at WAVRAN by an officer who will choose the site for the dump.

No. 5. WAVRAN DUMP. The following stores will be taken direct to WAVRAN:-
One blanket per man.   Canteen Stores.
Office Stores.   Mess Stores.
C.Q.M.S. Stores.

No. 6. BILLETING. Billeting party will consist of 2nd Lt. Bailey mounted & one signaller on bicycle. They will leave at 2-0 a.m.

No. 7. TRANSPORT. B.3 & C.3 will report at C.H.Q. at 9-0 a.m. D.3. at 9-30 a.m.

No. 8. BLANKETS. Section blanket rolls will consist of one blanket per man ONLY. The second blanket per man will be rolled separately to go to WAVRAN direct. All blankets to be at C.H.Q. by 7-30 a.m.

No. 9.
- A. If lorry has not arrived by 2-30 a.m. one signaller with bicycle will remain with Lieut. Cheesman.
- B. Officers valises will be at C.H.Q. by 8-45 a.m.
- C. Dinner will be served at ECLIMEUX at about 5-0 p.m.
- D. Billet Inspection at 2-15 a.m.
- E. Company will parade in front of C.H.Q.

Issued at 9-0 p.m. 16/11/17
to all concerned.

K.C. Springfield Capt.
O.C. 220th Machine Gun Coy.

330th MACHINE GUN COMPANY.

Move Order No. 5.

The Company will entrain at WAVRAN to-morrow.

Parade:- Coy will parade ready to march off at 1-30 p.m.

Dress. Full marching order. Carrying unexpended portion of days rations. Iron rations, full water bottles steel helmets, box respirators & gsd helmets. Leather Jerkins will not be worn, they will be carried on limbers.

Lorry. 1 lorry is allotted to the Coy.
A Signaller will report at Officers Mess at 8-30 a.m. ready to proceed to WAVRAN to act as guide for lorry, he will take a ration indent to the S.O. 30th Inf.Bde at WAVRANS STATION. This lorry will carry:-

Blankets rolled & labelled.
Horse rugs in rolls of 8.
Chemical containers.
Officers Mess Stores.
30 full cans of water & 30 sandbags.

These will be unloaded at Coy Dump at Station.
L/Cpl Williams & 2 men per section will form a permanent sanitary party & will proceed with this lorry. They will remain at the station and come under orders of Sergt. Sadler.
Further orders for this party will be issued later.
They will take two shovels, two picks & one broom.

Billets will be inspected at 1-15 p.m.
In future whenever the Coy vacates billets 1 N.C.O. & 1 man per billet will remain at billet till it has been inspected by either C.O. or 2nd i/c.

Water cart will march full.

S.A.A. limbers loaded as usual.

G.S. Waggon all Officers valises & C.Q.M.S.Stores.

Cooks Cart. Cooks Stores.

Issued at 7-45 p.m.
Nov.13th to all concerned.

E.O. Springfield Capt.
O.C. 330th Machine Gun Coy.

War Diary.

230th MACHINE GUN COMPANY.

Entrainment Orders.

The Coy will entrain on No.1: train from YAVRANS.
The following will be the probable accomodation available for the Coy, less vehicles.

```
16 covered trucks.
 1 1st class coach.
 1 3rd    "      "
```

8 covered trucks will be allotted to the transport.
6 trucks will each contain 8 horses or mules.
1 truck will contain 7 mules.
1 truck will contain 2 H.D. & 1 mule.
This last truck will contain 8 days forage as well.
Each truck will contain:-
Harness & saddlery of animals in the truck tied up in saddle
1 days forage drawn daily from forage truck.   blankets.
3 transport men in charge of animals.
Canvas buckets for watering.
All animals will be watered before entraining.
All animals will be entrained rugged.
Nos.3 & 4 Sections will form loading party to assist transport.Section under 2/Lieut.Costain. No other Officers or men will help to load animals without orders from C.O.
Throughout entrainment 2/Lt.Robinson will keep in close touch with C.O.
2/Lt.Robinson will report to A/RTO at 4-0 o'clock with entraining state in duplicate. This return will shew strength of Officers O.R. Animals, 4 wheeled & 2 wheeled vehicles, No.of days rations on train, Nos of Motorcars & motorcycles.
The CQMS will report to S.C. 30th I.B. at 4-0 oclock to draw 8 days train rations & forage.
No.2 Section will form a loading party to carry stores to trunk trucks under 2/Lt.Bleakley.
2/Lt.Bailey will be on the Station at 4-0 p.m. to chalk trucks shewing to whom allotted.
6 covered trucks will be reserved for men, 1 for rations and
1   "   "   for baggage.
1 compartment of 3rd class coach will be Coy Office.
1   "   "   "   "   "   "   " Servants
2   "   "   "   "   "   "   " for Sergeants.
1   "   "   "   "   "   "   " "Officers Mess Stores.
The Canteen will be in same covered truck as rations.
1 truck holds 35 O.R's.
2 R.A.M.C.Personnel will be on the train throughout journey.
No.1 Section will be in reserve under C.O. If any of this Section are detailed for duties, on completion of duty, they will at once report.back to section.
A spot will be picked where all Coy will pile arms and equipment before reporting for duty.
No.15 Section will provide a picquet of 4 men over these arms etc.
On arrival at Station a place will be allotted for Coy Cooks to prepar e tea. All dixies will be in charge of Cooks on H.Q. truck throughout journey.
The Transport waggons are being loaded by the Infantry.
Limber Corporals will remain by limbers until they are actually on the flats. They will make sure that the limbers are not interfered with. They will be held responsible that all bars supporting draught pole and swingle trees are placed in the front portions of their limbers and that all limbers are securely sheeted down.

www.ingramcontent.com/pod-product-compliance
Lightning Source LLC
Chambersburg PA
CBHW081238170426
43191CB00034B/1968